Hello, Family Members,

Learning to read is one of the most important accomplishments of early childhood. **Hello Reader!** books are designed to help children become skilled readers who like to read. Beginning readers learn to read by remembering frequently used words like "the," "is," and "and"; by using phonics skills to decode new words; and by interpreting picture and text clues. These books provide both the stories children enjoy and the structure they need to read fluently and independently. Here are suggestions for helping your child *before*, *during*, and *after* reading:

Before
- Look at the cover and pictures and have your child predict what the story is about.
- Read the story to your child.
- Encourage your child to chime in with familiar words and phrases.
- Echo read with your child by reading a line first and having your child read it after you do.

During
- Have your child think about a word he or she does not recognize right away. Provide hints such as "Let's see if we know the sounds" and "Have we read other words like this one?"
- Encourage your child to use phonics skills to sound out new words.
- Provide the word for your child when more assistance is needed so that he or she does not struggle and the experience of reading with you is a positive one.
- Encourage your child to have fun by reading with a lot of expression . . . like an actor!

After
- Have your child keep lists of interesting and favorite words.
- Encourage your child to read the books over and over again. Have him or her read to brothers, sisters, grandparents, and even teddy bears. Repeated readings develop confidence in young readers.
- Talk about the stories. Ask and answer questions. Share ideas about the funniest and most interesting characters and events in the stories.

I do hope that you and your child enjoy this book.

—Francie Alexander
Reading Specialist,
Scholastic's Learning

D1530851

For Remy

—M.O.

Go to scholastic.com for web site information on
Scholastic authors and illustrators.

ISBN 0-439-31705-3

Copyright © 2001 by Nancy Hall, Inc.
All rights reserved. Published by Scholastic Inc.
SCHOLASTIC, HELLO READER, CARTWHEEL BOOKS, and associated logos
are trademarks and/or registered trademarks of Scholastic Inc.

Library of Congress Cataloging-in-Publication Data

Olsen, Madeline.
    Johnny Appleseed / by Madeline Olsen; illustrated by Steven James Petruccio.
    p. cm. – (Hello reader! Level 1)
    ISBN 0-439-31705-3 (pbk.)
    1. Appleseed, Johnny, 1774-1845—Juvenile Literature. 2. Apple growers—United States—Biography—Juvenile Literature. 3. Frontier and pioneer life—Middle West—Juvenile Literature. [1. Appleseed, Johnny, 1774-1845. 2. Apple Growers. 3. Frontier and pioneer life.] I. Petruccio, Steven, ill. II. Title. III. Series.
    SB63.C46 B67 2001
    634'.11'092—dc21   2001020871
    [B]

10 9 8 7 6   02 03 04 05
                          Printed in the U.S.A.   24
                          First printing, September 2001

Johnny Appleseed

by Madeline Olsen
Illustrated by Steven James Petruccio

Hello Reader! — Level 1

SCHOLASTIC INC.

New York   Toronto   London   Auckland   Sydney
Mexico City   New Delhi   Hong Kong

This is the story of a man
who loved apples.
His name was John Chapman.
But he was called Johnny Appleseed.

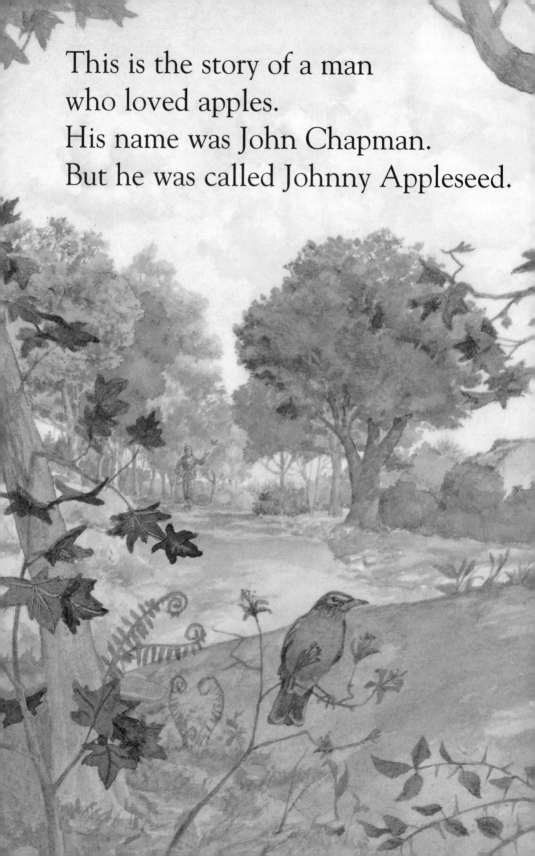

Johnny Appleseed loved to go
to new places.
He walked in woods.
He walked up and down hills.

And on his head he wore a pot.

Johnny loved the animals he met.
The animals came up close to him.
They were not afraid.

Johnny loved to be outdoors.
At night he sat by his fire.
He ate nuts and berries for dinner.

Most of all, Johnny Appleseed
loved apples.
He ate all kinds of apples—
red, yellow, and green.

Everywhere Johnny Appleseed
went, he planted apples.

He carried a sack filled
with apple seeds.
He helped people plant
the seeds in the ground.

First he worked hard
to clear the land.

Then he planted apple seeds.
The seeds were placed in rows.

He showed people
how to build fences.
The fences helped to keep out animals.
Now the seeds could grow.

Sometimes he gave people
small apple trees.
He showed the people
how to plant the trees.

Every spring the trees bloomed
with pink flowers.

In the fall the apples were ready
to be picked from the trees.

People made all kinds of delicious foods from the apples.
They ate applesauce and apple butter.
They drank cider.

Johnny Appleseed made
many friends.

Whenever Johnny visited,
the people welcomed him.

Johnny loved to talk with the children.
He told them stories.

Over the years, Johnny Appleseed
planted many trees.
He watched his trees grow tall.

Johnny wanted everyone
to enjoy apples.
That is why he shared
his apple seeds and trees.

Thanks to Johnny Appleseed,
today we enjoy many different kinds
of apples.

Golden Delicious
Russet
McIntosh
Rome Beauty
Jonathan
Fresh CIDER

The next time you eat an apple, think of Johnny Appleseed!